The Passion Play
2000
Oberammergau

Contents

One of the crosses on its way to be painted backstage

2000 – The 40th Season of the Oberammergau Passion Play

Christian Stückl

Every ten years, with the notable exceptions of 1770 and 1940, the villagers of Oberammergau have performed the Passion Play with great verve and, since time immemorial, the play has served as the stuff of controversies. In the year 2000, the villagers take to the stage for the fortieth time and, once again, act out the suffering and the death of the Nazarene.

The plot of the Oberammergau Passion Play has not changed since the first performance, 366 years ago: Christ's entry into Jerusalem, the Last Supper, the kiss of betrayal on the Mount of Olives, the mocking Roman soldiers, and the women who followed Christ to his crucifixion. Time and time again it is the same ritual: men and women let their hair grow for a year, the roles are cast, be they players or singers, and the young and old of the village go through a long and difficult series of rehearsals. Finally, in the summer of every tenth year, Jesus, Mary, Judas, John and Peter, the high priest Caiaphas, Pontius Pilate and the children of Jerusalem are called back to life. More than one hundred performances of the Passion Play are planned for this year. And so it has been, going right back to the time of the Thirty Years' War.

The director and producer Christian Stückl at the first reading of the text

The Beginnings

Amid the turmoil of the Thirty Years' War, the plague broke out in large parts of Europe, taking the lives of many more people than the war itself. The Black Death crept into the remote mountain valley at the foot of the Kofel where Oberammergau lies, in 1632. According to a chronicle of the time, the residents of the village set up a vigilant watch, and for a time they succeeded in keeping out the plague. During the annual fair held to commemorate the dedication of the village church, a man named Kaspar Schisler, who had worked outside the village during the summer, slipped over the mountains to his house in the village. Within a few days he succumbed to the plague – as did a large number of the people of Oberammergau.

In those days no one knew anything about germs, or the terrible toll they have exacted on humanity through the ages. People therefore invented incredible stories to explain the outbreak. They believed that the plague was spread by a green and yellow cloud that descended at night, or that Jews had poisoned the wells. And if there were no Jews in the village, then there was little doubt that God himself was sending the plague down from heaven to punish humanity for its sins. Often the people saw only one chance of survival: to pacify God's fury.

In 1633, devastated by the plague, the people of Oberammergau pledged to perform the Passion Play as a sign of their repentance and remorse over the suffering and death of Jesus Christ. Such vows were common at the time in many areas of Bavaria and Austria.

The chronicles relate further that from the day the people of Oberammergau gathered around the cross to swear their sacred vow, no further person died of the plague.

The first Passion Play of Oberammergau was staged in 1634. In 1680 the performance was moved to the first year of each decade. Were it not for the prohibition imposed in 1770 by the church and the state on the staging of passion plays in any form, and had the date for the Passion Play of 1940 not fallen during World War II, then there would never have been any interruptions in the history of the Passion Play.

The stage-set and costume designer Stefan Hageneier

The second director and dramaturgist Otto Huber

Why can't we let go of 'our' Passion?

In the year 2000, 1,600 adults and 550 children – more than ever before – are involved in the Passion Play.

Once again, the familiar story is retold: the story of Jesus of Nazareth. In his letter to the Hebrews, the apostle Paul writes that God "has spoken to us by a Son, whom he appointed the heir of all things, through whom also he created the world. He reflects the glory of God and bears the very stamp of his nature, upholding the universe by his word of power. When he had made purification for sins, he sat down at the right hand of the Majesty on high" (Hebrews 1:2–3).

It is the story of a Jewish man, a man of humble origins whose life ended horribly on a Roman cross, one of the most terrible instruments of torture ever invented. He died because he would not refrain from calling the religious leaders of his time hypocrites, rapacious wolves in sheeps' clothing, blindmen leading the blind; because he accused them of having turned the temple of God into a den of thieves, and of having murdered the prophets whom God sent to them. He died because he fought for his God and for his Jewish faith.

It is the story of Christ the Redeemer, whose resurrection from the dead set off a mighty movement – beginning with the Pentecostal sermon of the apostle Peter, the poor fisherman of Galilee, who became the representative of Jesus. It is he who spread His Church over the whole of the world.

It is the story of a man whose message has set worlds into motion for 2,000 years. Whose gospel helped the thousand of thousands go through the world, head held high, in freedom, professing their faith with pride. Spreading a message that shaped our culture and our way of life, that gave hope and strength for survival to countless oppressed and suffering people. A message that inspired Johann Sebastian Bach to compose the *St. Matthew Passion* and Leonardo da Vinci to paint the *Last Supper*.

But this is also the story of a man whose followers, the Christians, brought unbelievable suffering into the world. Their religious zeal recoiled from no act of violence, and left a bloody trail through the centuries. Millions of Jews – the people who shared the faith of Jesus – died in the twentieth century. They had to die because the church, and yes, the Passion Play for centuries sowed the seeds of anti-Semitism, of Jew-hating. The Nazis harvested a well-fertilized field.

We in Oberammergau enact the story of this man from his entry into Jerusalem to his death, from his last supper to the moment Mary Magdalene brings word of his resurrection to the disciples. We enact it at the end of the millennium, in the two-thousandth year since the birth of Jesus, at least according to our reckoning. In a time when the media predict the loss of all moral values, when it is fashionable to evoke the old story of the dance around the golden calf. We reenact it today, at a time when more and more Christians are renouncing both the Roman Catholic and the Protestant churches, at least in Europe. At a time when, knowing so much about scientific discoveries, we find it difficult if not impossible to believe in Mary's virgin birth or the physical resurrection of Jesus.

... and many more reasons

Nearly half of the residents of Oberammergau this year will come together on the stage of the Passion Play. They are Catholic and Protestant. Many among them have turned away from the Church altogether. This year, for the first time, some of the players will be drawn from among the Muslims who now live here. Children, barely potty-trained, will play alongside people in their nineties. The eldest among us are putting on our costumes for the eleventh time, counting the plays performed additionally in 1934, 1977 and 1984. How does a simple parish succeed in pulling off this kind of common project once every ten years? There can be no definitive answer. Too great are the differences among the players in personality, in religious orientation, in age and experience.

To many of us, the oath of our forefathers represents the beginning of a great theatrical tradition. To others it is a legacy, a solemn duty. In either case, a vow taken in the year 1633 is no longer binding on anyone. Many old traditions – indeed, many old passion play traditions – have disappeared. Yet Oberammergau still carries on.

Christian Stückl rehearses 'The Entry into Jerusalem' with the children

For many of the people of Oberammergau the religious act is the driving force behind the play. The dramaturgist Otto Huber, Second Director of the Passion Play 2000, wrote in 1990 that: "At the heart of the Passion Play, from the first enactment down to this day, we find an interpretation of the Passion

Stefan Hageneier and Inga Jäger, in charge of dressmaking, check a finished costume

of Jesus that is as simple as it is profound – a revelation of His love, of His absolute devotion to the Father and to Man. The passion plays can be understood as a school of love." In the mid-twentieth century Cardinal Faulhaber, the Archbishop of the Diocese of Munich and Friesing, bestowed upon the Passion Play a *missio canonica*: a church mission. Is the Passion Play a church service? Is it a mass, with the aim of perpetuating faith and love among the audience, of moving them to repent, to follow the word? Is Oberammergau the bastion of faith, an office of the church helping to mission the world?

In the end I must doubt that. Raising such a claim would be smug and foolish. Many of the players question their faith, as do many in the audience. Many players would never act as missionaries. Even in Oberammergau, there are those who have revoked their membership in the German Catholic Church. All the same, Oberammergau carries on.

Markus Zwink, the musical director, who adapted Dedler's work and added his own compositions, during orchestra practice

I believe the forces that bring the people of Oberammergau together every ten years are to be found in the story itself, the story of the man from Nazareth, and in the particular place where we tell that story: the theatre.

In his 1859 history of the village of Oberammergau the priest, theatre director and playwright, Josef Alois Daisenberger, wrote: "In general the Ammergauer is ... a friend of music and theatre."

I was seventeen when I first performed in the theatre in Oberammergau. Never in all the years have I encountered difficulties in casting. Seldom did a singer or musician reject the offer of a role. To my deep regret I sometimes maltreated a player during a rehearsal. But on the next day everyone was there again, all of us working towards a common goal: the performance, the premiere.

The people of this village like to get up on stage, and not just every tenth year. They love telling stories. They love the challenge of the script. The older, more experienced players let their voices resound, prodding the ambitions of the young. It is an honour to play Jesus or Mary. But the true theatre people are drawn to the theatrical roles – to the high priest Caiaphas, to the 'traitor' Judas. They await their costumes eagerly. They enjoy slipping into their roles.

The togetherness of a stage performance is seldom achieved outside the theatre. That is true of life's routine, in Oberammergau and everywhere else. When a nineteen-year-old acts for the first time in the role of a priest, an apostle, or a

Maria Buchwieser, the first female conductor ever during the history of the Oberammergau Passion Play

servant of Pilate, when he stands on stage together with a ninety-year-old player, when young and old sit next to each other in the dressing room, holding conversations across the generations, friendships are forged. A feeling of togetherness arises that often still vibrates with life many years hence.

All this does not always occur without friction. The people of Oberammergau tend to fight over their play. As long as I can remember, every Passion Play season was preceded by intense confrontations. Since the 1960s the script of the Passion Play has become a particular subject of controversy.

History of the Passion Play

The text has gone through many versions. From 1634 to 1860 ten different authors – usually clergymen from the monasteries at Rottenbuch or Ettal – revised, recast, or simply rewrote the script.

In 1750 Ferdinand Rosner, a Benedictine monk, created a grand reenactment, a drama between heaven and earth, between God and his adversary Lucifer. Jesus, sent by God to be His champion on Earth, triumphs over Death and the Devil. The hordes of Hell are hurled into the abyss.

The conductor Michael Bocklet at work with his orchestra

The Enlightenment banished the wild costumes, the earthy crudity, the blood and noise, the excesses and digressions associated with the play during the Baroque period.

In 1811 Othmar Weis, also a Benedictine monk, turned his back on the eighteenth-century script. His version concentrated instead on the gospels, on achieving a maximum possible realism, on the moral level. At the same time Rochus Dedler composed the music that, in altered form, is still performed during performances today.

The script was revised again by Joseph Alois Daisenberger for the play performed in 1860. Weis's realism gave way to grandeur and idealization. The audience was presented not with Jesus the man, but Christ, the Son of God.

Some innovations have been rewarded by time, others have been dropped. Every age has tried to give the never-changing story its own colour, its own interpretation. Each generation has tried to tell the story of the Nazarene in a fashion comprehensible to its own experiences, relevant to its own audience.

Putting the finishing touches to one of the olive trees

Theatre – a Scene of Confrontation

The twentieth century has broken with the tradition of living development, and turned preservation into a tradition. Various efforts to develop the Passion Play – including versions by Alois Johannes Lippl, Father Stephan Schaller, Carl Orff, and even an attempt to return to the Baroque play of Ferdinand Rosner, known as 'The Trial of 1977' – were nipped in the bud. Only in recent years has a readiness to regenerate and further develop the play gradually emerged.

The chief technician Carsten Lück, Christian Stückl, the theatrical sculptor Wolfgang van Elst, the set decorator Karl Witti and the stage designer Stefan Hageneier take a critical look one of the sets

Theatre witnesses constant shifts in emphasis. These are necessary. The stage is the scene of confrontation. Those who would make a museum of theatre only rob it of its life. In their hearts, the people of Oberammergau know this. In a referendum a majority voted in favour of revising the script by Othmar Weis and Joseph Alois Daisenberger, of setting the music to a new arrangement and of creating a new set and new costumes for the year 2000.

Preparations for the Passion Play 2000

Oberammergau has no permanent theatre operation. Every ten years it has to be established from scratch. Starting in March 1999 our local workshops engaged in a huge communal effort to create the 2,000 new costumes and twenty-eight new sets drawn up by the stage designer Stefan Hageneier. Many of the splendid fabrics that will be seen by the audience this year were purchased in India. The soldiers' weapons and armour were made by a blacksmith. More than six hundred costumes were tailored to individual players. Thousands of yards of material were dyed. Thousands of feathers had to be glued on. Tailors, carpenters, stage painters, sculptors and lighting technicians worked together in creating, for the first time in seventy years, a new look for the Passion Play 2000.

The Passion Play features 130 speaking roles. Two players are cast for each of the nineteen major parts which include Jesus, Mary, John, Judas, Caiaphas and Pilate. The younger and less experienced actors are given elocution lessons and voice training. At the weekends, almost 1,000 adults and 550 children gather on the open stage to sing *Heil dir, o Davidsohn* (Hail to Thee, Oh Son of David), with which the people of Jerusalem greet Jesus on his entry and practice the scene in which Pilate delivers his judgement. A choir of 120 singers and the Passion Play orchestra rehearse the music composed by Rochus Dedler in a new arrangement by the musical director Markus Zwink.

Carola von Klier adds some more colour to one of the costumes with a paint gun

All this is to bring the 'greatest story ever told' to the stage. It is the story of a faithful Jew who set out to recover what he felt the people had lost: justice, compassion and faith; who held contempt for all who wore their piety like festive costumes; who was ready to be stripped naked, maltreated and mocked before howling crowds for his God; and who stayed steady on his path to its final consequence – to his execution on the cross.

"And all the multitudes who assembled to see the sight, when they saw what had taken place, returned home beating their breasts" (Luke 23:48). With these words the Gospel of Luke concludes its story of the passion. Perhaps we shall succeed, in the year 2000, on the stage of the Passion Play Theatre, in calling forth the form of Jesus of Nazareth to confront the audience in a way hitherto unseen.

Chorus and Prologue

A chorus and Prologue guide the audience through a play the content of which is summed up by Paul – in one of the earliest formulations of the Christian faith – with the words: "... he humbled himself and became obedient to death, even death on a cross" (Philippians 2:8).

If, however, all that were told on the stage at Oberammergau was how Jesus of Nazareth was plunged into disaster and put to death, this story would hardly differ from the countless tragedies that we encounter every day. But there is another side to Jesus's Passion, to which Paul refers in the very next sentence: "Therefore God exalted him to the highest place and gave him the name that is above every name, that at the name of Jesus every knee should bow, in heaven and on earth and under the earth, and every tongue confess that Jesus Christ is Lord, to the glory of God the Father" (Philippians 2:9).

It is the task of the chorus and Prologue at Oberammergau to lead spectators from all over the world to recognise this second, mysterious aspect of the Passion. And to help them comprehend that God's reality shines out from this man who dies, helpless, on the cross, the scenes are preceded by moments from the religious history of Israel presented in the form of tableaux. These tableaux show prophets who, sent out into a world that was always more or less remote from God, even anti-God, suffered disaster too. But they also make us aware how, time and again, people experienced the saving intervention of the God of Israel at their moment of greatest need. They thus help us to accept trustingly something that is beyond our understanding: that it is in the direst catastrophe, when suffering plumbs the very depths of hell, that God's benevolence towards mankind becomes apparent.

Prologue: Jesus reopens the gate to life that was shut against Adam

"Mankind is banned from Eden's meadows ..." The chorus laments that we no longer live in Paradise, in close proximity to God, where everything was freely available to men and women, where the relationship with God and with our own kind was happy, and guilt, hatred, sorrow and death were unknown. Mankind did not, so to speak, fall in with God's grandiose design.

The closeness to God that has been lost is restored in Jesus. In him we can see what men and women could be, how with increasing closeness to God there is a concomitant increase in humanity, justice, openness and fullness of life, as well as a growth in creative power that bursts all the bounds of traditional ideas. Jesus's example also demonstrates how a person who places "all his worldly goods" in God will not be disappointed but will gain a life that exceeds time and space.

He who promised that he would be with us "always, even until the end of the world", that he would accompany us "through thick and thin", stands large before us. At the start of a play that shows us how, viewed superficially, his commitment to God and mankind led to his fall, he reminds us: I know from the inside the terrible things that you are about to see and that in one way or another darken the lives of people for all time, and in the end I conquered them. "Death, where is thy sting? Hell, where is thy victory?"

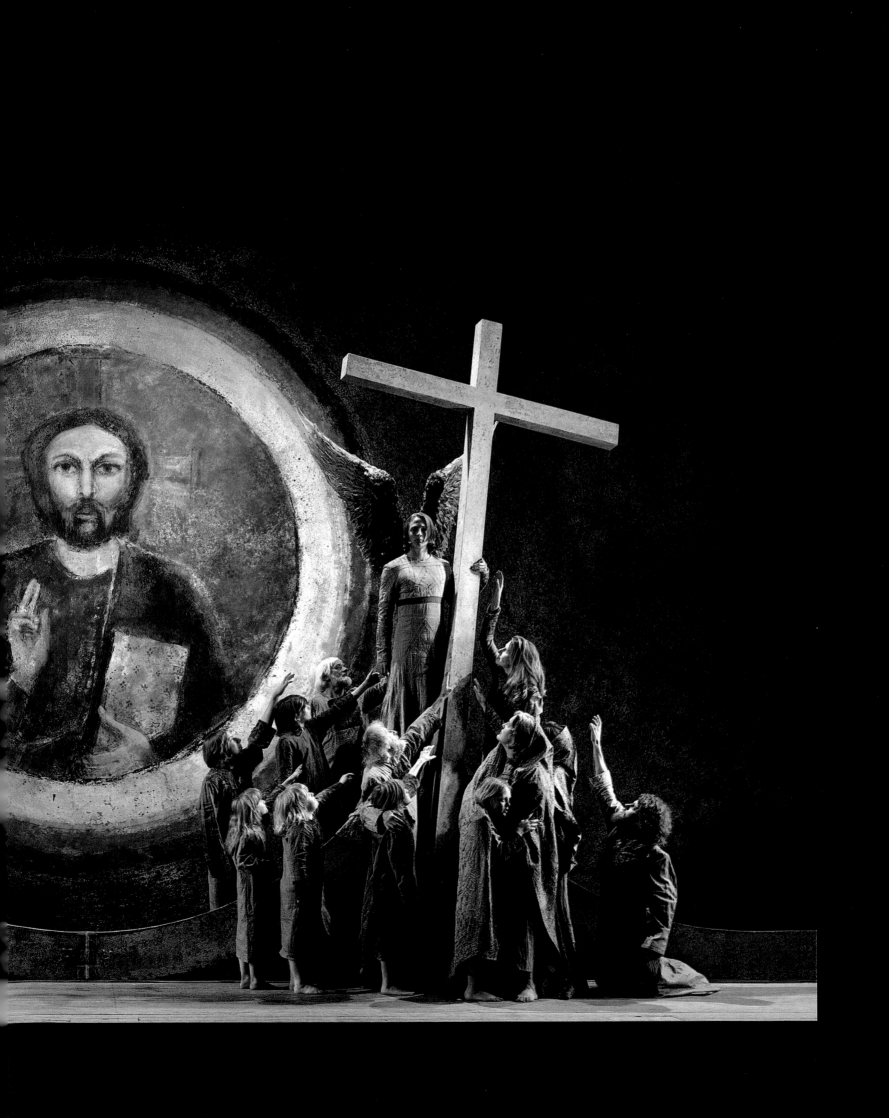

Entry into Jerusalem

Pilgrims from all over the country make their way to Jerusalem. It is the time of the Passover feast, held to commemorate Israel's deliverance from Egypt. Among the pilgrims is Jesus of Nazareth, coming from Jericho in the company of friends and disciples.

Jerusalem is an uneasy city. People are yearning to be set free, as the Israelites had been from Egypt in times past. Since the local religious leaders, half-rebellious, half-collaborating, are barely able to hold their ground against the Roman occupation forces, political hopes focus on men from the ordinary folk. People are keeping a look-out for some emissary from God, someone who, according to the old Messianic beliefs, will restore the splendour of his covenanted people, Israel.

Jesus, whose reputation for unusual deeds, as well as unusual benevolence, has raced ahead of him, is regarded by many as this bearer of hope. The populace greet him with rejoicing when he enters the city, riding not on a "high horse" like some Caesar but on a donkey, just as the prophet Zachariah had once foretold the arrival of the Prince of Peace. The people spread garments out before the new king and wave victory palms. Has he not revealed himself through miracles? Has he not entered the city via the Mount of Olives, from where the Lord's Anointed is expected to come?

His route takes him to the heart of the city, the temple. In line with his call, "Strive first for the kingdom of God!", Jesus, in a prophetic gesture, brushes aside everything that bars the view of God, or God's house, unconcerned by normal practice and the customary rights of the traders, much to the jubilation of the ordinary folk and children with whom he says a prayer in front of the cleared temple. He then calls out to them: "You are the salt of the earth! You are the light of the world!"

For the foreign political rulers and the religious dignitaries and their associates it must seem like a total reversal of values when Jesus exhorts them to "Become like children!" Is this because the latter appear to him to be more full of life? More open? Less imbued with the sense of their own importance than with trust in God's fatherly providence? At any rate, Jesus thereby provokes the representatives of power and order, Roman and Jewish alike, as though challenging them to reach a decision.

Jesus drives the money changers
from the temple

Prayer in the temple

Jesus and the children

In Bethany

Jesus goes to Bethany, a village close to Jerusalem. Here, too, we see an alternation between those moments when addressing the people in public and those times spent in the circle of close friends. It is typical that one of the houses he visits is Simon, whom he cured of leprosy, and Lazarus, whom he raised from the dead. Few of his circle of friends, however, have any personal experience of him restoring a person's health or of bringing someone back to life.

The controversy aroused by his appearance at the temple penetrates even as far as Bethany. Who is he? What gives him authority? Is he merely arousing empty hopes? Peter answers the key question: "You are the Messiah". His declaration means, "God is close to us in you". Exactly this, to pass on the message of God's closeness, is what Jesus demands of his friends, sending them out "as sheep among wolves".

A woman approaches Jesus and anoints him with precious spikenard oil worth an entire year's wages. Through her action she becomes the exemplar of a boundlessly extravagant love, giving up everything for Jesus, yet several people express their lack of comprehension. Would not the money have been better invested in helping the poor or in safeguarding her own livelihood?

Jesus's explanation that "she did it to prepare me for burial" draws attention to the violent death that awaits him and wrests his friends out of their dreams of his political triumph, rapidly reversing the circumstances.

The extent to which Jesus sees his return to Jerusalem as a divine task becomes clear when he rejects Peter's wish (that he remove himself to a safe place) as an idea from Satan.

In the Passion Play, Jesus's setting out on this path is preceded by a tableau showing the departure of Tobias. Tobias's father Tobit, a pious man who is, however, unhappy in his faith – has sunk into a state of depression, expressed in his going blind. Led by an angel, Tobias sets out from this darkened world on a journey from which he will bring back good fortune to his family: a healing remedy for his father's eyes, a wife for himself and the pecuniary means for an existence free of care for all of them. Even if the significance of the way ahead is not always clear to Jesus, as on the Mount of Olives, he is nevertheless unable to imagine that it will bring mankind anything other than salvation, since he sees himself as the vehicle for God's redeeming care.

In Bethany

Mary Magdalene anoints Jesus

Judas calls for support for the poor

"Get out of my sight! You are not judging by God's standards, but by human standards"

Parting

The disciples try to stop Jesus from risking his life, as do his brothers, who have followed him from Galilee together with his mother Mary. From the words of his relatives, as from those of Judas, the theme of anxiety emerges. How are we to come to grips with life? Without you? As though, without the trust in God that radiates from Jesus everyday life will fall down on them like a ton of bricks. They are consumed by their fear. We are reminded of the story of the furious storm on the Sea of Galilee when the disciples were frightened to death but Jesus slept. Or of the words from the epistle to the Philippians: "Let your gentleness be evident to all. The Lord is near. Do not be anxious about anything, but in everything, by prayer and petition, with thanksgiving, present your requests to God" (Philippians 4:5–6). When God is near, near in Jesus, people seem to be relieved of an oppressive anxiety, freed to do good.

Nothing is said in the gospels about Jesus taking leave of his mother, apart from the farewell at the Cross reported in St John's Gospel. But this scene, which pious imagination has liked to picture, must have taken place somewhere. In line with episodes involving Mary in the gospels, the Passion Play makes two things evident here. Her life too seems to be crossed; the parting, her loss, cause her pain. On the other hand she finds the mental strength to assent and to let go of her son.

To make the connection to Mary, Mary Magdalene and all the others who loved Jesus, the parting scene is preceded by an unusual tableau taken from one of the greatest love poems in literature, the *Song of Songs*. The bride is plunged from the heights of happy love into grief and despair when she no longer finds her lover by her side and she seeks him through all the streets of the city.

Supplementing the perspective of hope given in the earlier Tobias tableau, this tableau portrays the other side of parting: the pain, loneliness and unhappiness of those who are separated. Yet, when following the bride's laments, her friends console her by promising that her beloved will return, this is an advance pointer to the Easter reunion of those who have been separated. The risen Christ, however, is no longer physically limited to meeting just one or other of his close friends and relatives, but offers himself universally to every human being as a loving listener, a companion through life and a mediator with God.

His mother and brothers meet Jesus in Bethany

Again in Front of the Temple

Jesus goes back to the temple with a great number of followers, mostly people who have little to lose but hope, through him, to gain everything. His words are no less radical than on his first appearance there. Even merely the first of his beatitudes: "Blessed are the poor in spirit, for theirs is the kingdom of heaven", is of a radical that has hardly been matched to date. If Jesus calls a person blessed who places all his future hopes in God, then why have Christians set into the world so many stone, military or financial bastions of their own power, instead of taking God as their "rock and refuge"?

The political realist Caiaphas, a member of the aristocratic Sadducees and a man accustomed to owe his future to his own political machinations, also finds Jesus's ideas more than disconcerting. Was it not through successful diplomacy and tactics that his father-in-law and master Annas, after first obtaining the position of high priest for himself, was able to manoeuvre three of his sons into office? And what has it not cost him, Caiaphas, how many favours, before he so ingratiated himself with the Roman exploiter Pilate that the latter heaved him into office – always bearing in mind that he has managed to achieve this without totally losing the semblance of loyalty and adherence to tradition among his own people? And all this, including the still moderate level of cruelty and violence by the occupation troops, is now to be thrown into jeopardy by a political nobody?

As opposed to such calculated thinking, Jesus proclaims quite simply that everything depends on the relationship to the One above. He demands goodness, which is important to God, and he attacks the practice of religion that focuses on the practitioner's own interest: a public criticism to which, eventually, the authorities react by clearing the area. Jesus thereby places himself in the tradition of the Jewish prophets, one of whom is depicted in the preceding tableau. When Moses comes down from Mount Sinai with the tablets from God and sees the people dancing around the golden calf, he demands they decide whether to serve God or the idol of their own power.

Jesus encounters resistance, as each of the prophets did. Although there is some dissent, Caiaphas manages to establish the view among the council members that an end must be put to Jesus's actions, which he sees as troublemaking. Judas enters. Disappointed by Jesus, whose announcement of his imminent sufferings had struck him like a declaration of bankruptcy, he offers his

The priests try to get the
support of the populace

Jesus admonishes the high priest

Caiaphas clears the temple

Caiaphas demands the death penalty for Jesus

Judas receives 30 pieces of silver

Nicodemus defends Jesus

The evening of the Passover feast approaches. In just the same way as expectations of love and harmony are often associated with Christmas nowadays and those who feel their lives lacking frequently become depressed, so it is too before this Passover feast – combined with the hope that the will of God shall prove victorious – Jesus's disciples are bewildered, disappointed and despondent. Has it all been in vain? Have Jesus's commitment and their own efforts on his behalf (for whose sake they have neglected everything else) been unsuccessful?

Jesus does not offer them any soothing words. On the contrary, he conjures up the possibility of a world that will turn its back on God completely and lapse into absolute inhumanity. "Because of the increase of wickedness, the love of most will grow cold" (Matthew 24:12). In view of this danger in particular Jesus asks for compassion towards the needy, the hungry, the imprisoned. The disciples' request to show them the Father, he does something that is usually a servant's job when guests enter the house: he washes their feet.

And he invites them to join him in the festive supper. He says the traditional Haggadah prayers with them. But when, during the course of this ritual ceremony, it is time to break the bread and bless the wine, Jesus gives these traditional gestures a completely new turn. Looking ahead to his imminent death, he offers himself, his own life, in the bread and wine in order to become one with his friends in such a way that nothing, not even his death, can separate them.

But this meal is also overshadowed by a tragic rift. "As soon as Judas had taken the bread, he went out. And it was night" (John 13:30).

The tableau before the last meal that Jesus will share with his disciples is of the dramatic Passover meal that the Israelites celebrated the night before their exodus from Egypt: that time of mortal danger from the Egyptian authorities a lamb is sacrificed and the Israelites hope for their God's saving, liberating intervention. The angel passes by, protecting the families whose doors are marked with the blood of the Passover lamb. This experience of the saviour God of Israel also forms the foundation of Jesus's faith in the hour when his life is at stake and he himself becomes the Passover lamb.

"I yearn to celebrate this Passover meal with you"

The washing of feet

The last supper

"Drink! My blood!"

"Whatever you wish to do, do it soon!"

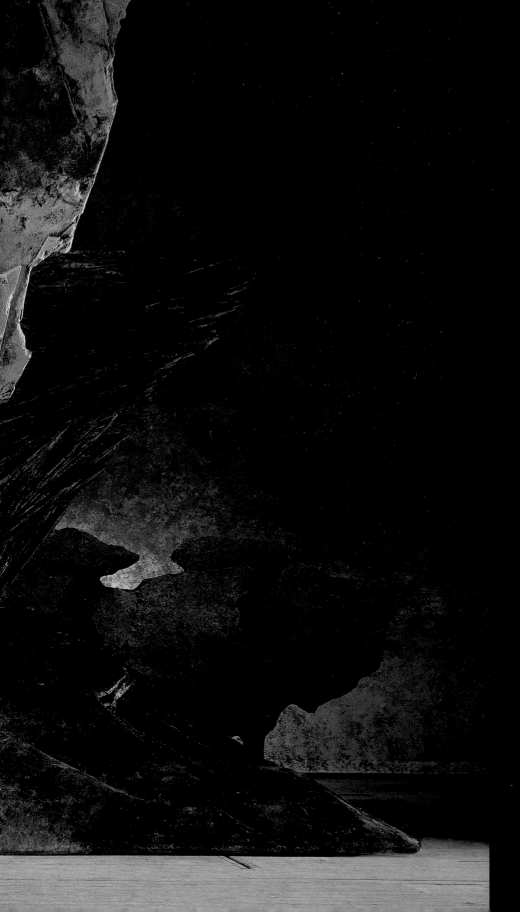

On the Mount of Olives

After the festive supper Jesus and his disciples go to the Mount of Olives. He prepares them for the deep crisis of faith that lies ahead of them: "... for it is written, 'I will strike the shepherd, and the sheep of the flock will be scattered'" (Matthew 26:31). Peter's boastful words, "Even if all fall away on account of you, I never will", do not deceive Jesus. He foresees that Peter, in particular, will betray him.

The irrevocable decision is reached among the olive trees of Gethsemane. In his mind Jesus experiences in advance his death at Golgotha, as is suggested in the Epistle to the Hebrews: "During the days of Jesus' life on earth, he offered up prayers and petitions with loud cries and tears to the one who could save him from death ..." (Hebrews 5:7). As Mark states, Jesus began to be "deeply distressed and troubled". He prays in the words of Psalm 42:

"As the deer pants for streams of water, / so my soul pants for you, O God. / [...]
My tears have been my food day and night, / while men say to me all day long, / 'Where is your God?' / [...]
My soul is downcast within me; / [...] all your waves and breakers / have swept over me."

Jesus, who taught his disciples the Lord's Prayer, pledge "Your will be done", now himself beseeches "If it is possible, may this cup be taken from me" (Matthew 26:39). Although he immediately adds "Yet not as I will, but as you will", it is obvious how very much he is tempted here – a temptation which turns his sweat to blood and which awake and praying, he wrestles with himself to overcome, while his disciples sleep.

An angel appears and consoles him. "Take upon yourself the ills of mankind! Let yourself be pierced by their crimes, crushed by their sins. Heal them through your wounds. I make you a light for the peoples, so that my salvation reaches even to the ends of the earth."

The tableau that precedes this episode on the Mount of Olives portrays the moment when Moses hears the voice of God from the burning thorn bush commanding him to go to Pharaoh and demand that he set Israel free. Moses feels this is asking too much of him and initially resists the task until, with the revelation of the name of God, Yahwe, he receives the pledge that God will be with him.

"Father, do not desert me"

"Simon, you are sleeping"

"I make you into the light for the nations"

Again and again in the life of Jesus there are moments of dramatic tension, whether this is his first contentious appearance in the local synagogue in his home town of Nazareth, or his entry through the gates of Jerusalem – the start of the escalation of the controversy surrounding him and simultaneously the start of a new era in the history of mankind. The temptation of Jesus on the Mount of Olives, where the drama is played out internally, in the mind, is followed by an externally turbulent scene with the arrival of the soldiers led by Judas.

The scene begins with Judas's kiss, gesture of greeting which was customary when greeting one's teacher, but which, as a symbol of intimacy and affection, contrasts starkly with the fact that here it is used to make Jesus known to his enemies. He who entered Jerusalem riding on a donkey as the Prince of Peace is now arrested like a criminal. Jesus first makes sure his disciples' lives are safe: "If it is me you seek, then let these others go". When Peter draws his sword and injures one of the soldiers, Jesus tells him to put his sword away: "All they that take the sword shall perish with the sword". This brings to the fore a theme that has already been introduced physically when the arresting party marched in, equipped with swords and staves, and will run like a constant thread throughout the remainder of the Passion story: the question of violence or force and how it can be overcome. In viewing the Passion, we should bear in mind the question posed by the 19th-century German dramatist Georg Büchner: "What is it in us which lies, whores, steals and kills?" A question that needs to be asked with even greater urgency in light of the atrocities of the twentieth century.

The arrest on the Mount of Olives also represents a sort of break in the action, since from this point onwards Jesus hardly says another word, as though he feels it impossible in principle to make himself understood by those now assailing him. Moreover, the things that we see seem like the visible, surface movements of events that are taking place subliminally, hidden from view. The forces that are at work here are indicated when Jesus says to Peter, "Shall I not drink the cup the Father has given me?" (John 18:11), or to those who have come to arrest him, "This is your hour – when darkness reigns" (Luke 22:53). Matching the theme of violence, the preceding tableau shows an act of revenge between army commanders. Joab, one of David's commanders, and his rival Amasa meet with their forces at the cliffs of Gibeon. They greet each other with a kiss, in feigned friendship, but Joab uses this physical proximity to stab Amasa to death with a dagger.

Pages 70/71: "Rabbi, greetings to you!"

Kiss and arrest

Interrogation before Annas

Taken into custody, led away, presented for questioning – events follow in quick succession. The wheels of the machinery start to turn, and from the outset one has the impression that the process is unstoppable. Jesus is already undergoing a sort of preliminary interrogation before Annas, the "éminence grise".

Asked in a roundabout way about his disciples and his teaching, Jesus replies: "I have spoken openly to the world, I always taught in synagogues or at the temple. I said nothing in secret. Why question me? Ask those who heard me. They know what I said." The meaning of these words is that his whole life has been directed to revealing the truth, although only a person who, believing in him, is ready to receive it, will grasp what remains hidden from someone such as Annas.

Not understanding Jesus's cryptic answer and believing it to be disrespectful – and something for which Jesus has to be punished – Annas's servant hits him and, in so doing, puts himself in the wrong. In this gesture in which, for the first time Jesus is hurt physically, we see how an established power has a tendency to react when it feels its authority is being questioned: with violence. Prophetic figures, from Isaiah down to the martyrs of the Third Reich, have experienced this time and time again and – as the cases of Joan of Arc, Juan de la Cruz and many others demonstrate – from Christian authorities too.

When Jesus first spoke in public in Nazareth and met with rejection, he said: "Only in his home town and in his own house is a prophet without honour" (Matthew 13:57). Here and later his words reveal that he sees himself as a prophet, charged with the task of telling people about God and about how human life should be lived according to God's ideas, even if often they shut their ears to this message. This – and not, as is popularly believed, foreseeing the future – was the task of prophets.

One of the greatest of the latter, Moses, appears in several tableaux in the Passion Play. Before the start of the present episode of extreme distress and unjust accusations, however, we see a tableau of the prophet Daniel, thrown into the lions' den because he is accused of holding firm to his faith and continuing to pray to the God of Israel. Just like Daniel, Jesus does not yield or relinquish his point of view, defying all charges laid against him. God is with him too in the deepest abyss, like the angel was with Daniel.

Jesus is slapped in the face
before the high priest Annas

Mockery – Peter's Betrayal and Remorse

After being questioned by Annas, Jesus becomes the object of his guards' mocking games. They are probably afraid of him, since he is said to have prophetic gifts, and cover this up by outdoing each other in inventing 'bold' provocations and testing Jesus's powers as a seer in a coarse and brutal variation of blind man's buff. But why does Jesus remain silent?

Taking an example from the 20th century, a former inmate of the Dachau concentration camp once reported of an SS man who would regularly read a work by the great philosopher Spinoza during his breaks but, when he was in charge, behaved no more humanely than the other guards. As present-day trials of war criminals also demonstrate, the urge to use brute force takes on a life of its own within certain groups or in certain circumstances. Perhaps it is because Jesus knows this that he hardly utters a word of protest against the injustice of his tormentors. Nevertheless, he does say to the one who strikes him with his fist under Annas's gaze: "But I told the truth. Why do you hit me?"

The preceding tableau shows Job in misery – the archetype of the suffering human being. The chorus provides a commentary with the words: "Yet he bears his afflictions patiently. / Beset on all sides by scorn and derision / he trusts, hoping, in his God. / No word of complaint issues from him."

Christians have often taken Jesus's silent endurance of injustice as an example to themselves. And of course there is an underlying reason that should be heeded. Jesus refrains from complaining about injustice or seeking retaliation himself because he knows that every retaliation entails new injustice in a never-ending cycle. Instead he leaves it to his father to bring about justice, even offering the soldier who struck him his other cheek. Certainly, such willingness to absorb the evil in the world has often contributed to peace and brought stability to communities. However, although it is not an infrequent occurance that people act out their suppressed aggression on others, all too often they are silent, especially in the face of injustices committed by 'the powers that be' – referring here, in particular, to the wrongs done to Jesus's people in the Third Reich.

In complete contrast to Jesus's action, this scene shows Peter's concern to avoid suffering through denial. This enables Peter to save his own life but does not make him happy.

The soldiers mock Jesus

"You are one of the disciples of the Galilean"

Peter, surrounded by soldiers, betrays Jesus

"What a miserable person I am! How low have I fallen!"

Interrogation before Caiaphas – Judas's Despair

In God's Name is the title of a book that accused the Vatican of pursuing financial and political, even criminal, goals under the guise of religious interests. As the title indicates, we react with disappointment and indignation when religion, something normally considered sacrosanct, is used as an instrument for other ends.

Caiaphas, to whom Jesus is now brought, is an exceedingly dubious figure in this respect. In order to rid society of the troublemaker, Jesus, he not only exploits the religious laws (so that many people of later ages believed the Torah as such brought about Jesus's downfall), but also flouts the law. He organises a hearing at night – despite the fact that this is banned – and held, not in the official premises of the Sanhedrin, the council, but in his own palace! He does not permit any witnesses to speak for the defence and – according to one theory – does not even invite all 70 council members, some of whom might vote for Jesus, but only the 'apparatchiks' who are under his thumb. Nevertheless, objections are raised in Jesus's favour: "He is not accused of anything that would merit the death sentence", or: "In his own way, although you condemn it, he serves the God of our fathers. He believes in everything that is written in law and in the prophets and has the same hope in God as many of us here." Caiaphas ignores these objections and is sufficiently cunning to prevent any official verdict, since this would have a shaky foundation. For a start, only the Romans have the legal authority to pronounce a death sentence.

Judas's plea to hand back the person he delivered up to them does not receive a hearing. He is alone with his guilt.

Nobody will ever know why he betrayed Jesus. The ridiculous sum of 30 pieces of silver cannot have been the motive. Was he disappointed that there was no political revolution? Did he want to test Jesus, force him to give proof of his power? In any case, was he not ultimately merely an instrument of God's plan for the salvation of the world? One thing is certain: Judas hangs himself even before Jesus dies on the cross.

The tableau that precedes the despairing Judas depicts the despairing Cain. Both of them judge themselves and act hastily, forestalling God's mercy, thanks to which – so Jesus teaches – there is always another chance.

Interrogation before Caiaphas

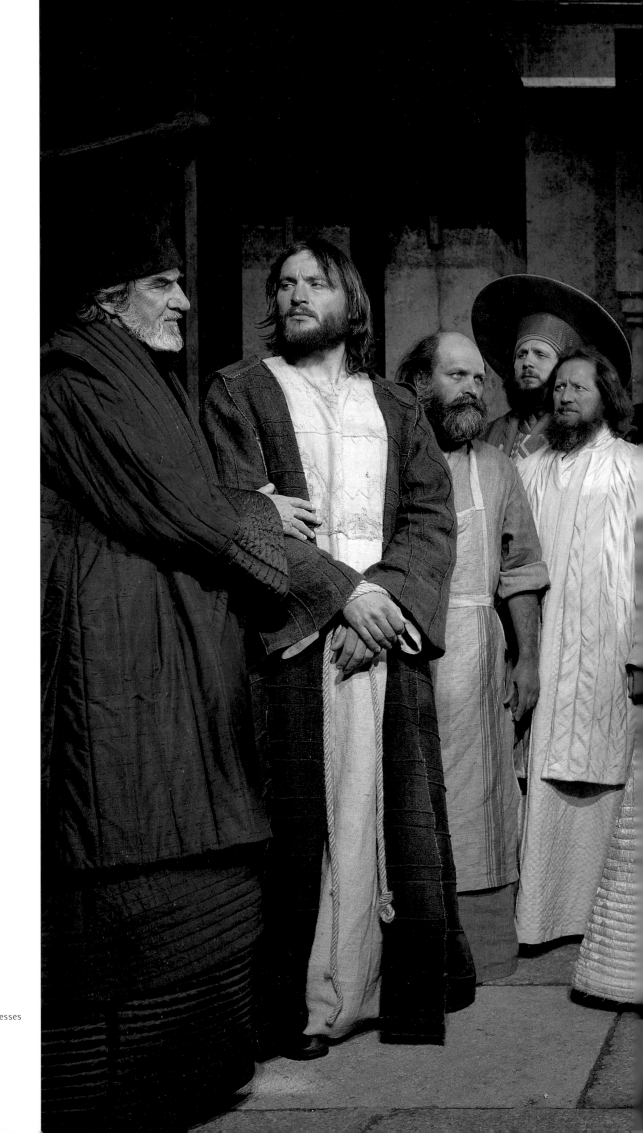

Hearing of witnesses

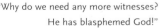

"Why do we need any more witnesses?
He has blasphemed God!"

Judas asks for Jesus to be let free   Judas kills himself

Jesus is handed over to Pilate, the Roman governor of Judea. "Venality, violence, unlawful appropriation of property, continued executions without legal proceedings, incessant and unbearable cruelty": these are just some of the accusations made against him by his contemporary Philo. Although Luke 13:1 reports that Pilate had Galilean pilgrims butchered in the temple, the gospels are otherwise kind to the image of this man of power, who looks to his own advantage without consideration for others. This is even true of the relationship with his minion Caiaphas, whose own ambitions he mistrusts. He is not hesitating to convict Jesus out of sympathy but because he does not wish to do Caiaphas any favours. And also because of diplomatic caution: questions of religion are outside his remit and his reputation in Rome is already damaged (because of his excesses he will later be removed from office). In addition he makes a miscalculation, hoping that if he offers Jesus as an alternative to Barabbas within the terms of the Passover amnesty he will be able to keep Barabbas, politically the more dangerous of the two, in prison. There is no basis whatsoever in law for him to have Jesus flogged.

In Jesus he is faced with his absolute opposite, someone who represents new laws in human relationships – a realm in which God's benevolence towards mankind will be fulfilled. Pilate, however, dismisses Jesus's claim with a shrug of his shoulders and the negligent query "What is truth?".

The tableau before this encounter is of the scene in which Moses tells Pharaoh: "This is what the Lord, the God of Israel, says: 'Let my people go'". And Pharaoh replies: "Who is the Lord, that I should obey him and let Israel go? I do not know the Lord" (Exodus 5:1–2). In both cases a power system – as also happened not infrequently in the twentieth century – cuts itself off from a reality that would call its own standards into question.

Jesus's appearance before Herod Antipas is a bizarre interlude. Politically of little weight – he is not even king, but tetrarch, of a small region under Roman rule – and barely recognised by the people because of his non-Jewish descent, Herod lives a life of dissipation devoted to his love of magnificence and passion for building. A king fit for an operetta! Having had John the Baptist put to death, he suspects that Jesus is John returned from the dead. Once this fear is put to rest, he asks Jesus to perform some sensational miracle as a sign. Not unlike some people of our own age, he is able only to comprehend the world as a spectacle, as a consumer item.

"What is truth?"

Jesus is turned over to Pontius Pilate

Herod mocks Jesus

... and calls him the king of fools

Flogged ...

... crowned with thorns

Ecce homo

Pontius Pilate Condemns Jesus to Death

Without first determining Jesus's guilt in keeping with standard legal proceedings, and without even having the right to detain him, Pilate offers his 'release' as part of the Passover amnesty when the people are allowed to choose one person to be set free. The crafty tactician knows that he, a Roman, has no chance of mobilising the mob to pick the one – Jesus – whom he wants because of his complete insignificance on the political front. But Pilate does expect an overwhelming sympathy vote for Jesus and hopes, by pardoning him, to put himself in a favourable light with the people and be able to keep Barabbas locked up.

"But the chief priests stirred up the crowd to have Pilate release Barabbas instead" (Mark 15:11) – against the opposition of Jesus's followers. Even if the high priests managed to persuade their claqueurs to take part in the demonstration, perhaps by dubious means, it requires a special demagogic zeal to tilt the crowd's mood in favour of Barabbas. Soon indeed it no longer seems to be about Jesus, but merely a question of giving the hated occupier a metaphorical kick in the teeth.

Where in such a confused tangle of interests can justice be found? It seems an absurd and alien concept here. Where is credibility, when all legal channels compromise themselves, both the state-appointed judge – who grotesquely washes his fingers 'in innocence' of Jesus's blood – and the crowd? The 'voice of the people': who here can still believe it to be the 'voice of God'? As when called before the People's Court in Nazi Germany, all and every hope for humanity and justice is in vain, where a whirlpool of violence and counter-violence, ideology and counter-ideology spins ever more quickly until finally someone is put to death, it is as though hell itself were glaring back at us from the eye of such a maelstrom. And one must feel astonishment at the blindness of the spectators of 1934, who did not recognise this scene as a mirror of their own circumstances.

This moment in which Jesus sinks ever closer to rock-bottom and becomes ever less recognisable as the bringer of salvation, sent from God, is preceded by a tableau of Joseph as the epitome of a radiant man of God, a saviour elevated to splendour. The tableau exposes the contradictions. Can God's voice be present in somebody who remains silent? Can we expect help from somebody who was not even able to help himself?

Crowds gather in the streets

Jesus or Barabbas?   Pontius Pilate washes his hands

... and sentences him to death on the cross

On the Way of the Cross

John brings Mary the news that Jesus has been flogged. Flogging is the preliminary stage to crucifixion, so everybody knows what his fate is.

After sentencing, a cross is laid on Jesus's shoulders, as people condemned to death had to carry the instrument of their execution to the actual site. He has to carry it before the eyes of the city in order to make it plain he no longer has anything to do with them. Like a person with an infectious disease, he is expelled from the community.

Physical aspects force their way into the foreground: the heat, the soldiers' shouted orders, laughter, the cries of the others being taken with him to Golgotha, the sweat running into his eyes, the weeping wounds, the pounding in his ears … He falls to the ground and is pulled back on to his feet.

More shouts, crowd noises, now swelling, now receding, faces staring at him in shock or astonishment. Among them suddenly is the face, the familiar features, of his mother. More blows on his back, which he no longer feels very much, then the shouts fade, the faces go dark. Again he is lying on the ground. The soldiers force a stranger, accompanied by his sons, to carry the cross for him.

Of his twelve disciples he sees only John – the shepherd is struck down and the sheep of the flock are scattered. The spectators keep their distance, as when the secret police take somebody away. Surely he must have done something wrong for this to happen. A group of women step closer, lamenting, weeping for him. He says: "Do not weep for me; weep for yourselves and for your children. For a time will come when people will say to the mountains, 'Fall on us!', and to the hills, 'Cover us!' For if men do these things when the tree is green, what will happen when it is dry"?

A woman hands him a cloth so that he can wipe his face. She will remember his dirty, bloody face. And Christians will remember it whenever they look into a dirty, bloody face.

The preceding tableau portrays Isaac. His father Abraham believed he had to sacrifice his beloved son on Mount Moria, as commanded by his inscrutable God. Isaac himself carried up the mountain the wood for the fire on which he was to be burnt. The story of this absolute trust in God ends with God revealing that what matters to him is not human sacrifice but a heart that is prepared to give itself completely to him. As in the case of Jesus.

"You will not be able to bear the sight of him!"

Mary meets her son

Simon of Cyrene is forced to carry the cross

Veronica hands him the cloth

raised so that they are suspended above the heads of the people, between heaven and earth.

Above Jesus's head is a notice inscribed with the charge against him: "Jesus of Nazareth, King of the Jews". The Roman authorities understand the Jewish concept of the Messiah, the Lord's Anointed, only as a claim to royal powers. The notice gives rise to doubts, mockery, arguments, which continue to the present day. A powerless king? His kingdom a whim or reality? The slow, agonising death begins. And the soldiers while away the time, dividing up the condemned men's belongings.

Mary and John approach the cross. Jesus places the mother whom he is leaving into the care of John as another "son", founding a community to which – after Easter – countless more will flock.

"Eloi, Eloi, lama sabachthani! My God, my God, why have you forsaken me?" Jesus cries, the initial words of a Jewish psalm which veers between deepest despair and hope: "... I am a worm and not a man, scorned by men and despised by the people./[...] You who fear the Lord, praise him!/[...] For he has not despised or disdained the suffering of the afflicted one;/he has not hidden his face from him but has listened to his cry for help" (Psalm 22). Jesus is alone, deserted. He does not feel his Father's hands, into which he commits his spirit. Then "Jesus breathed his last" (Mark 15:37).

To ensure he is dead, Longinus pierces his side with a spear, "bringing a sudden flow of blood and water" (John 19:34). "Thus Jesus's heart remains open through all eternity, in order to refresh with the mysterious living source that gushes forth from him all those who labour and are heavy laden" (Urs von Balthasar, adpt.). Nicodemus and Joseph of Arimathea take Jesus down from the cross and lay him in his mother's lap. Finally they lay him to rest in a rock tomb.

The preceding tableau takes as its central theme the relationship to the cross. Just as the Israelites, mortally wounded by snake bites, were healed by gazing upon the metal snake that Moses set up on a pole, so whoever gazes at Jesus on the cross gains strength to live.

Jesus is nailed to the cross

"Woman, see your son!"

"If you are the Messiah, come down from the cross!"

"My God, why have you forsaken me?"

Longinus pierces his side with a spear

Deposition

Pietà

Soldiers guard the grave until the third day

"He is not in the grave"

"Woman, why are you weeping? He has arisen from the dead!"

Mary Magdalene spreads the word of the resurrection

The lamb is slain.
The earth enfolds the Holy One.

But weeping and pain,
sadness and lamentation will flee,

For the Lord casts death
into the flaming inferno,

And He will crush
the serpent's head!

He frees his beloved son
from the prison of death.

Forcefully he breaks open the gate.
Out of the darkness of night

the Lord's Anointed arises in majesty
and brilliant light

And leads us to the source
From which life's waters course.

Prologue to the Resurrection

"I am with you always until the end of the world"

The Actors and Actresses

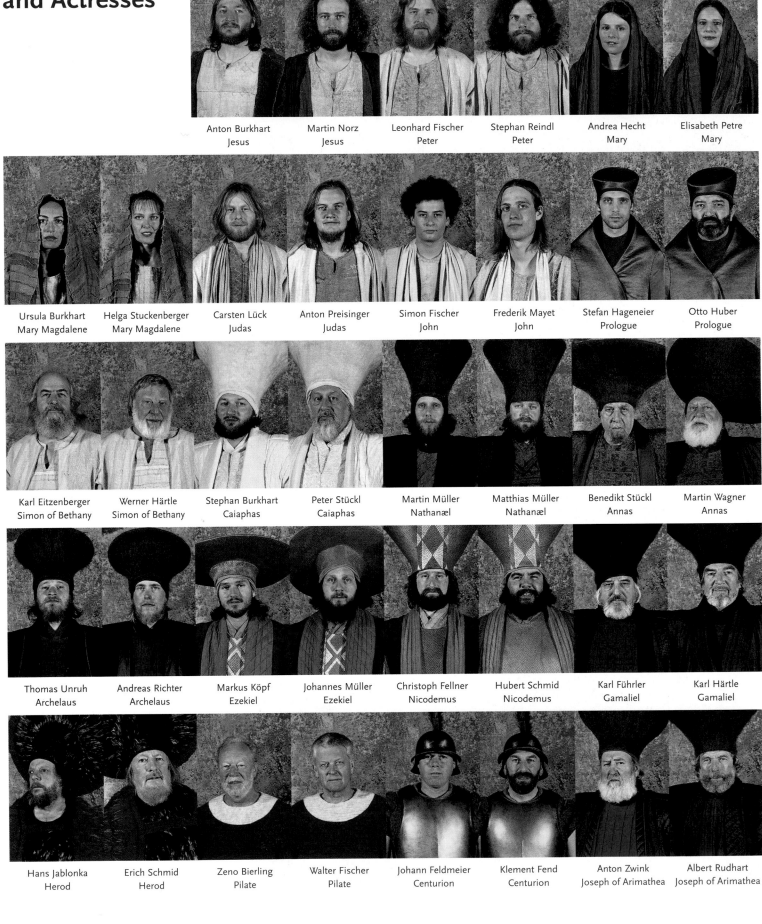

Anton Burkhart
Jesus

Martin Norz
Jesus

Leonhard Fischer
Peter

Stephan Reindl
Peter

Andrea Hecht
Mary

Elisabeth Petre
Mary

Ursula Burkhart
Mary Magdalene

Helga Stuckenberger
Mary Magdalene

Carsten Lück
Judas

Anton Preisinger
Judas

Simon Fischer
John

Frederik Mayet
John

Stefan Hageneier
Prologue

Otto Huber
Prologue

Karl Eitzenberger
Simon of Bethany

Werner Härtle
Simon of Bethany

Stephan Burkhart
Caiaphas

Peter Stückl
Caiaphas

Martin Müller
Nathanæl

Matthias Müller
Nathanæl

Benedikt Stückl
Annas

Martin Wagner
Annas

Thomas Unruh
Archelaus

Andreas Richter
Archelaus

Markus Köpf
Ezekiel

Johannes Müller
Ezekiel

Christoph Fellner
Nicodemus

Hubert Schmid
Nicodemus

Karl Führler
Gamaliel

Karl Härtle
Gamaliel

Hans Jablonka
Herod

Erich Schmid
Herod

Zeno Bierling
Pilate

Walter Fischer
Pilate

Johann Feldmeier
Centurion

Klement Fend
Centurion

Anton Zwink
Joseph of Arimathea

Albert Rudhart
Joseph of Arimathea

In the oldest surviving records in Oberammergau an entry for the period from September 1632 until October 1633 lists the names of eighty plague victims.

The prologue in the earliest existing manuscript of the text from 1662, with a Protestant introduction: "Salvation and mercy from God alone ..."

The Oberammergau Passion Play: a Chronology

Otto Huber

1633   In the beginning was the vow... After the Thirty Years War, the Black Death spread rapidly, reaching Oberammergau in 1632. By October of the following year eighty deaths had already been recorded. The Chronicle of that time reported how "... at this time of suffering the village councils of the Six and the Twelve met and vowed to perform the Passion Play every ten years, and from this time on not a single person more died." Since the Parish Elders had declined to take the vow, the Passion Play is still traditionally supervised by the local council. At that time, the Catholic reform movement actively encouraged displays of piety. Between 1600 and 1650, there were approximately forty different villages where passion plays were performed in Bavaria and Austria alone, and over 250 in the period from 1550 to 1800 as a whole.

Passion plays, first performed in the 12th century as demonstrations of devout piety, reenact the suffering and death of Jesus of Nazareth, the Redeemer, and have always been portrayed with a great depth of emotion. Plays were initially performed in the larger cities throughout Europe and covered scenes taken from the Bible ranging from the expulsion of Adam from Paradise, to the Resurrection of Jesus Christ. After passing their zenith at the end of the 15th century, passion plays disappeared from the cities. Criticism in favour of rationalistic theology contributed to this change, just as much a general degeneration in the standard of the plays. In Catholic southern Germany and Austria, the passion play enjoyed a renewed popularity from the 16th to the 18th centuries. It was to become a mass medium for the Catholic reform movement, although performances were held very rarely in cities but in rural communities instead.

1634   The first performance of the Oberammergau Passion Play. "The play of the suffering, death, and resurrection of our Lord Jesus Christ" is reenacted at Whitsun by sixty to seventy performers in the graveyard next to the church.

1662   The Oberammergau schoolmaster, Georg Kaiser, records the text used for the Passion Play, providing us with the oldest surviving script. He notes that the text has been revised, indicating that the versions used for performances held in 1634, 1644, and 1654 are similiar, although changes have often been made to the script over a period of many years.

Even the oldest text, comprising 4,902 verses, is itself adapted from that of two older plays:

The first is a Catholic passion play dating from the latter half of the 15th century, the manuscript of which had been found in the Benedictine Monastery of St. Ulrich and Afra in Augsburg. This play in turn is based on one performed in the Tyrol (a region in modern-day Austria) as well as medieval writings on the Passion.

The second is the *Tragedi* Passion of 1566 by Sebastian Wild, Mastersinger of Augsburg. This was inspired by reformist principles and, since the text had actually been published, it was widely known. Wild, in turn, used the humanist play *Christus redividus* (1543) by the Oxford reformer Nicholas Grimald, as a model.

From the very outset, the Oberammergau tradition never drew on the naive, but was based on a carefully structured, theologically founded, ecumenical text.

1674   The fifth Passion Play, following performances in 1634, 1644, 1654, and 1664. Scenes from the *Weilheim Passion* (1600, 1615) by the parish priest Johannes Älbl are added. The *Weilheim Passion* originated from a group of late mediaeval Alemannic Passion Plays dating from the 15th and 16th centuries. Scenes from the Passion are accompanied by music.

1680   The sixth Passion Play. The date for the performance of the Play is changed to the first year of every decade – the reason for this, however, is unknown.

1690   The seventh Passion Play. An entry in the earliest surviving accounts sheets mentions that "a total cost of 45 florins, 45 Kreuzer has been incurred" as a result of the performance.

1700   The eighth Passion Play. Accounting records cite expenditure for costumes borrowed from Rottenbuch Monastery and "an honorarium for the trumpeters from Ettal."

1710   The ninth Passion Play. The play is directed by Father Thomas Ainhaus who also makes improvements to the rhyming verse.

1720   The tenth Passion Play. Surviving sections of the text revised by Father Karl Bader of Ettal (1662–1731), indicate a Baroque stage with wings.

1730   The eleventh Passion Play. The text is adapted by the Augustinian canon Anselm Manhardt (1680–1752) of Rottenbuch, who introduces Satan and the allegorical figures of Hell – Jealousy, Avarice, Sin, and Death – as enemies of Jesus, and expands the traditional, meditative and artistic device of 'freezing' the action into a series of motionless tableaux vivants. There are two performances causing a total debt of 84 florins.

1740   The twelfth Passion Play. The text is revised by Clemens Prasser (1703–1770), vicar of Oberammergau and later provost of Rottenbuch. The play was probably performed twice.

1750   The thirteenth Passion Play. Responding to criticism voiced in the Age of Reason that the most sacred story of Christianity had no place on a stage, the villagers in Oberammergau seek a new form of presentation. An eloquent and pious scriptwriter is found in the person of the Benedictine monk Ferdinand Rosner (1709–1778) of Ettal, who pulls

The Benedictine monk, Father Ferdinand Rosner (1709–1778) of Ettal, professor of rhetoric at the Ettal Knights' Academy, and author of the *Passio nova* of 1750, entitled 'Wretched Suffering, Victorious Death and Glorious Resurrection of the Son of God made Man.'

One of the oldest costumes worn in the Passion Play: the magnificent, richly embroidered gown worn by the high priest, Caiaphas (2nd half of the 18th century).

The Benedictine monk, Father Othmar Weis (1769–1843) of Ettal who, in his texts on the Passion, reacted to changes in the theatre and to the theology of his time, and contributed to the survival of this genre in the 19th century.

Rochus Dedler (1779–1822), a teacher and composer born in Oberammergau, wrote the music to accompany Othmar Weis's text for the Passion Plays in 1811, 1815 and 1820. Since no authentic portrait of Dedler exists, the artist M. Z. Diemer painted this imaginary portrait in 1920, based on contemporary descriptions.

all the registers of the sacred Baroque theater in the 8,457 verses of his *Passio nova*.

Jealousy, avarice, sin and death are personified in the play which places Jesus in the centre of a dramatic struggle between the philanthropy of God and the powers of Evil.

The performance is divided by seven musically accompanied 'Observations' comprising three tableaux vivants in each instance. In motionless pictures the actors present archetypal scenes from the Old Testament and the parables of Jesus Christ. They tell the story of Jesus, focussing on the Passion which superficially appears as a catastrophe, as a redeeming act of God.

Rosner's text gains in popularity in Bavaria, and the Oberammergau Passion Play becomes a model for performances in other places.

1760   The fourteenth Passion Play. Two performances attended by 14,000 spectators.

1770   No performance is held. An appeal for special permission is rejected in spite of repeated efforts.
        In a bold petition, the villages point out that "from twenty, thirty or more miles around, from Bavaria, Tyrol, Swabia and the Realm, from the cities of Munich, Freysing, Landshut, Innsbruck, Augsburg and other places, it is not only the simple burgher and farming stock but also the gentry and learned persons who take it upon themselves to visit the spectacle, and many extol their satisfaction and always with great pleasure, more than they had indeed hoped. None of the scenes or characters are at all laughable, puerile or lacking in taste and the principal roles are performed by men who have travelled far and wide throughout Europe, and who well know what is to be considered low and abhorent in other places and what is desirous for such a sacred performance."
        There is no income to balance the costs incurred for the preparations, resulting in a massive deficit of 274 fl.

1780   The fifteenth Passion Play. Oberammergau is the only village whose request to perform a passion play is granted. A version of Rosner's script, revised by the Benedictine monk Magnus Knipfelberger (1747–1825) of Ettal, is performed three times. Entitled "The Old and New Testament," it excludes the theme of the Passion.

1790   The sixteenth Passion Play. Permission for five performances is granted and is seen by a total of 11,000 spectators. The Play gains its first mention in a newspaper and tickets are issued for the first time. The village makes a profit of 600 fl.

1800   The seventeenth Passion Play. Renewed permission. The Napoleonic Wars result in a reduction of spectators to approximately 3000, which means the village council has to contribute 205 fl.

1801   The eighteenth Passion Play. In order to reduce the debt the village incurred due to the wars, special permission is given to perform the Passion of 1800 four times.

1810   A letter by Minister Count Maximilian Montgelas revokes the permission granted to Oberammergau, so there are no performances.

1811   The nineteenth Passion Play. Permission is granted to perform, after the submission of a new text by Dr. Othmar Weis (1769–1843), priest of Ettal. This text concentrates on the gospels, eliminates legendary, mythological, allegorical and lyrical elements, introduces contemporary theology, prose style, realism, and wordy, moralising interpretations of the tableaux, reference to social conflicts and the central idea of atonement.
The music is composed by Rochus Dedler (1779–1822), a teacher from Oberammergau. Even today, this music still lends the Passion Play its character.

1815   The twentieth Passion Play. Special performances after the end of the Napoleonic Wars.
Further extensive revision of the text by Weis and of the music by Dedler (continues until 1820): expansion of the crowd scenes, including the 'Entry into Jerusalem'). A new stage is built in the Empire Style by Father Johann Nikolaus Unhoch (1762–1832), with a broad proscenium and a changeable central stage, flanked by two-storey 'houses,' 'alleyways' leading off to the sides and arcades. As a consequence the scenery is renewed.
Members of the government and nobility attend, including Minister Montgelas, feared for his prohibition to hold performances in previous years.

1820   The twenty-first Passion Play. The first eye-witness account of the performance of this Passion Play in Oberammergau survives. In it, the royal planning officer Anton Baumgartner describes the text, the stage and scenery, as well as the performers and the music.

1830   The twenty-second Passion Play. King Ludwig I grants special permission for the Play to be performed, under the condition that the stage no

longer be erected in the graveyard. The stage, which had been used since 1815, is reerected in a meadow on the north-west edge of the village. This ground plan still determines the structure of the theatre today. 5,000 spectators can be accommodated.

However, only 13,000 visitors attend the dress rehearsal and 10 performances.

An letter written to Goethe by Sulpice Boisserée in which he enthusiastically talks about the Oberammergau Passion Play, is published by Goethe in the periodical 'Chaos.'

1840 The twenty-third Passion Play. 35,000 people attend. The increase in spectators is due to accounts written by celebrated visitors to the Passion Play in 1820 and 1830 who discovered and publicised it from a Romantic viewpoint.

1850 The twenty-fourth Passion Play. The parish priest of Oberammergau, Joseph Alois Daisenberger (1799–1883), is appointed to direct the Play. In the spirit of his teacher, Johann Michael Sailer, the learned theologian, historian and man of letters is very active in educating the people and publishes a number of his own historical and dramatic works. 464 actors perform in front of a total of some 45,000 spectators. Reports by famous visitors describe the Oberammergau Passion Play as a national heritage based on an idealized picture of the Middle Ages, a 'precious relic of a bygone Germany' and a 'sanctuary of the German spirit.'
First French and English reports on the Play.

1860 The twenty-fifth Passion Play. Daisenberger revises the text at the government's request, taking account of the criticism made in 1850. He creates a text that is classical in character and historical in its reference to elements from classical antiquity and German tragedy, as well as incorporating elements from earlier passion plays. He aims at timelessness instead of the updating preferred by Weis, at idealisation instead of realism and at the psychological element instead of the political. For example, Judas is no longer presented as the generally

The advisor on spiritual matters and reformer of the Passion Play: Joseph Alois Daisenberger (1799–1883), who also directed the play from 1850 to 1870, photographed here in the summer of 1871 by Steigenberger and Johannes, Weilheim.

Early photographs taken in 1871 by Jakob Steigenberger, Weilheim.
left: Jesus (Joseph Mayr) is anointed by Mary Magdalene
right: the executioner's assistants throw dice for Jesus's cloak

despised greedy devil, but as a doubter, full of worry and fears of being expelled from the heavenly realm. Daisenberger prefers stylization, weaves in leitmotivs and likes to play with ideas. His use of symbols such as light and darkness corresponds to his preference for the Gospel of St. John.

On the other hand, he attempts to add popularity by the incorporation of legends (Veronica, Ahasuerus) and incidents on the Way of the Cross (Jesus meeting with Mary), by the use of old Passion texts, by warm-heartedness, vivid language and simple symbols (the Cross as the Tree of Life).

Some 10,000 spectators including King Maximillian II, writers such as Hans Christian Andersen, and many church officials attend a total of 21 performances.

1870   The twenty-sixth Passion Play. Daisenberger writes prologues to the tableaux vivants in classical ode metres, clothes the texts in blank verse and tries to give the script the flavour of a work of the German classical age. However, with the exception of the prologue, his proposal was not accepted by the village.

1871   Continuation of the twenty-sixth Passion Play, after interruption by the war with France.

"May the Play, this inheritance of a Germany of yore, witness our brethren from the north and the south united in love as citizens of a reborne Germany" – such was the announcement for the Oberammergau Passion Play in the periodical 'Germania.' Many of the estimated 40,000 visitors come from England (including Crown Prince Edward) and the United States. Many celebrities attend (such as Richard Wagner), as well as members of the aristocracy. A command performance is given for King Ludwig II, who donates a group of monumental figures portraying the cruxifixion scene. At his request, court photographer Joseph Albert takes pictures of all the tableaux and of various scenes after the performance.

Pilate's costume in the historical 'Meininger' style, made for the Play in 1880 with the assistance of the costume department at the theatre in the royal palace in Munich.

right: 1910, 'The Entry into Jerusalem' on the stage rebuilt for the 1890 season. The central section was designed as a Corinthian temple. (Photo by H. Traut, 1910)

below: the new auditorium under construction for the 1900 season. The roof is structured around six huge, arched, iron girders.

bottom: the completed structure accommodates 4,200 spectators. The wall at the opposite end to the stage was painted with rustic and historical motifs.

1880   The twenty-seventh Passion Play. As in Wagner's Festival Hall in Bayreuth the orchestra pit is deepened to be out of the audience's line of sight. Roofs are added to the loges at the back, and a gallery is added around the theatre for standing room. Elaborate new scenery is made and – in cooperation with the Munich Court Theatre – new costumes, particularly for the principal figures such as Pilate.
The extension of the railway to Murnau makes travelling that much easier and the London-based travel agency, Thomas Cook, introduces revolutionary forms of organised tourism. Similar to that on religious festivals, the flood of visitors is a sign of self-assertion by the Church in its struggle with the State under Bismarck.
Among the spectators are the composer Anton Bruckner and Duke Georg II von Sachsen-Meiningen who played an important role in establishing an historical theatrical genre. 100,000 spectators.

1890   The twenty-eighth Passion Play. The stage is rebuilt by the internationally renowned Munich theatre technician Carl Lautenschläger, director of the stage machinery at the Munich Court Theatre. It is "a worthy representative structure full of atmosphere" in the neo-Renaissance style, incorporating state-of-the-art technology. By moving Anna's and Pilate's houses and their external staircases to either side of the stage, a new area is created to accommodate crowd scenes. A glazed roof over the central section permits natural light to enter but makes it necessary for the backdrops to be raised from below instead – a feature found nowhere else in the world. Complex technical machinery is introduced to create the illusion of clouds, thunder, lightening, angels' wings, etc. 124,000 visitors attend 40 performances.

1900   The twenty-ninth Passion Play. Anton Lang's passionate performance as Jesus from 1900–22 greatly influences the Play. The 4,200-seat auditorium is now covered by an iron girder roof-construction with six high arches, open at one end to the stage which remains exposed to the elements.

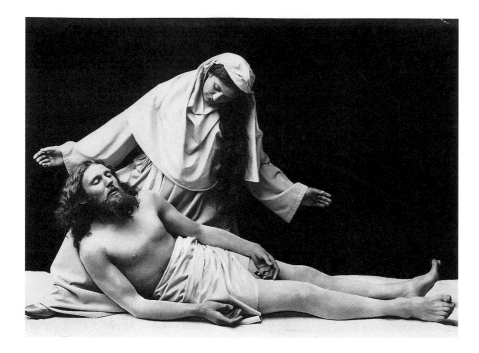

'The Lamentation of the Body of Christ' (Anton Lang) with Mary (Anna Flunger) in 1900. (Photo by Leo Schweyer, Stuttgart). Directed by Johann Evangelist Lang who was mayor of Oberammergau at that time.

An 'Official Book of the Text' is published by the village council for the first time.

"Oberammergau welcomes guests from around the globe; even three gentlemen from China," declares the headline in the local newspaper. The donation box in the church contains coins from Egypt, India, Hong Kong, America, Mexico, Brasilia, Bolivia and Peru. The list of prominent spectators reads like a 'Who's who?' of the time. It includes crowned heads of state from Russia, France, Sweden, England, Italy, Austro-Hungary, Saxony, Prussia and Denmark, "unbelievably wealthy Americans" such as Rockefeller and Vanderbilt, "English sufragettes," Auguste Eiffel, Count Zeppelin, poets, artists, names from the stage, innumerable heads of the church from as far afield as New York and Australia, and Cardinal Ratti, later to become Pope Pius XI.

A bibliography of publications on Oberammergau includes 150 titles, many of which are of regional interest and around a dozen are works of literature. The most famous of these is Ludwig Ganghofer's *Der Herrgottschnitzer von Ammergau,* a best-seller that is adapted for the stage and contributes to the increase in popularity and significance of folk and peasant theatre. *Am Kreuz*, an Oberammergau Passion novel by author Hermine von Hillern, causes a scandal and is censored.

The Catholic Teachers' Association in Bavaria celebrates the survival of the Church in a secular world with a centenary festival. Oberammergau becomes the symbol of conservative values and is idealized by followers of related art forms. A Catholic literary theoretician maintains that the Catholic culture is based on two principles: Athens (= idealism) and Oberammergau (= faith in its most resolute form). 174,000 spectators.

The sculptor, Georg Johann Lang (1889–1968; left), director of the Plays from 1922 until 1960, and his brother, the architect Raimund Lang (1895–1976; right), mayor of Oberammergau 1933–45/1950–66, during a planning meeting for the remodelling of the Passion Play Theatre for the 1930 season.

1910   The thirtieth Passion Play. A total of 223,548 visitors attend 56 performances. On the eve of the outbreak of World War I the Play has a unique effect on the audience. The number of visitors is similar to that in 1900.

Sketch for set design, Crucifixion scene, in a modern – and, at the time –revolutionary, new stage production. Georg Johann Langs (1930)

1922   The thirty-first Passion Play. The aftermath of war results in the Play being postponed by two years.
A new beginning is made and the young sculptor Georg Johann Lang (1889–1968) is chosen to direct the Play. The response exceeds all expectations: Instead of the 31 planned performances, 67 had to be given to accommodate 311,127 visitors, including 100,000 from abroad. Although inflation eliminates any profit, lucrative offers from film companies are turned down.

1930   The thirty-second Passion Play. The new staging by Georg Johann Lang is the first performance to implement truly modern directive methods. The strict minimalism of the sets is matched by an artistic concentration and an impressive handling of crowd scenes. Instead of using the historical set of 1890, a financial risk is taken and a simple, ascetic, monumental stage is constructed. The architect is Raimund Lang, who is later to become mayor of Oberammergau.
Visitors include the British Prime Minister Sir Ramsay MacDonald, Henry Ford and Rabindranath Tagore. The seating area is extended to accommodate 5,200 spectators.

1934   The thirty-third Passion Play. Special performances on the occasion of the 300th jubilee. The price of the tickets is reduced quite dramatically

'The Crucifixion' for the 1930 season. (Photo: Friedrich Bauer, 1930)

and special train fares are offered. The new powers-that-be call for the motto 'Germany is calling you!' to be added to the posters and an attempt is made to monopolize the ideological element of the 'farmers' play,' coming from the 'blessed power of the earth'. Shortly before the general election is held, Hitler takes advantage of Oberammergau's popularity by visiting the village himself.

The Catholic church grants Oberammergau the *Missio canonica* – the official teaching permit. 440,000 visitors. Leo Weismantel (1888–1964) is commisioned to revise the text, but the commission is later withdrawn due to objections raised by the conservative fraction.

1940   The Play is not performed due to the war. Preparations, which had been started in 1938 following a declaration by the Ministry for Propaganda that the Play was 'important to the Reich,' were disbanded.

1950   The thirty-fourth Passion Play. The performances in 1950 are conditioned by the catastrophic situation in Germany. This is, however, seen as an opportunity for presenting the country in a different light, namely that of a country embedded in the Western Christian tradition.
Performances are held in front of an unexpectedly large number of international visitors, many of whom had attended previously. At the same time an exhibition is staged entitled '1,000 Years of Christian Art in the Sign of the Passion.'
Members of Parliament who attend include the first President of the German Federal Republic, Theodor Heuss and the Chancellor, Konrad Adenauer. The highest ranking representative of the Allied Forces at the Play is Dwight D. Eisenhower. 480,000 visitors attend an extended run of 87 performances (33 were planned). Dedler's music is revised by Prof. Eugen Papst (1886–1956) who was born in Oberammergau.

1960   The thirty-fifth Passion Play. Georg Johann Lang, directing the play for the last time, looks for writers (e.g. Alois Johannes Lippl and Arthur

Deposition. From the cycle of etchings Hans Schwaighofer – For a New Oberammergau Passion Play, shown at the exhibition of the same name in the Foyer of the Bayerischer Rundfunk in Munich (1970)

Jesus is condemned by Pontius Pilate (Rosner trial performance, 1977; director: Hans Schwaighofer

Maximilian Miller) who are able to come up with a theologically and artistically contemporary script appropriate to the times, but his efforts are in vain. Thus the production from 1930 is put on with hardly any changes.

Both Christian and Jewish critics claim that Judaism is portrayed in a negative light. The Abbot of Ettal, Dr. Johannes Maria Höck, makes minor corrections to the text as a consequence. Approximately 500,000 visitors attend.

1970 The thirty-sixth Passion Play. During a period receptive to reform (not only on account of the *Vaticanum II*), there is a growing wish both within Oberammergau and elsewhere to revise the Play. The text has been changed little since 1870 and the production itself has hardly been modifed since 1930. In 1961, the community of Oberammergau initiates a discussion with theologians and artists. Carl Orff's sugges-tion of a return to the Rosner text from 1750 is taken up and rehearsals take place under Hans Schwaighofer who had presented his ideas for staging the Play back in 1967. However, when the final decision is made to use the Daisenberger text again in 1970, Schwaighofer steps down. Father Stephan Schaller of Ettal is commissioned to rework the Daisenberger text. His version, designed to convey a more modern message, is not accepted by the council in 1969, although certain details are indeed incorporated in a corrected version issued by the committee responsible for the text. Despite Cardinal Döpfner's assur-ance that the Play did not address the question of an individual guilt or a collective guilt on the part of the Jews, but rather a failure of both modern-day Israel and the Church, the anti-Jewish debate did not diminish. In America, it even led to a boycott of the Play by Jewish organizations.

Anton Preisinger (1912–1989) directs the Lang version with very few changes. With more than 530,000 visitors attending 102 performances, the conservative fraction feels that its stance has been confirmed.

1980 The thirty-seventh Passion Play. The Catholic Academy within the diocese of Munich-Freising supports Oberammergau in its search for a reform and, in 1973, organizes a symposium entitled 'The Passion Play in Today's Age.' In 1973, a similar event under the heading 'The Passion of Christ as a Religious Play' is attended by the film director Franco Zeffirelli, among others, and representatives of the Jewish faith.

In 1975, the council commissions Hans Schwaighofer to direct a trial performance of the Play using Rosner's text. Based on the fascinating work with its allegorical figures and dramatic concept of salvation (see 1750), Schwaighofer devises the stage sets, masks and costumes, Alois Fink the stage adaptation and the composer, Wolfgang Fortner, the music. In 1977, after seven months of rehearsals involving seven hundred actors, the play is performed eight times and is extremely positively received by the public. However, following a survey, the majority vote against the Rosner text for 1980. At first the council is in favour of Rosner, but a newly elected council decides on the Weis–Daisenberger text shortly afterwards should be used for the 1980 Play.

In 1978 the Anti-Defamation League, a Jewish organisation founded in 1913 to combat anti-Semitism, participates in the discussion. The League assigns the Catholic theologians Leonard Swidler and Gerald Sloyen the task of identifying the problems with the Passion text. Father Gregor Rümmelein and new director Hans Maier revise the text, taking Swidler's and Sloyen's criticism into account. Maier also revises most of Lang's sets for the 1980 production.

All 18 leading roles are cast with two performers of equal status. The number of seats is reduced to 4,700. (460,000 people attend).

1984   The thirty-eighth Passion Play. Approximately 480,000 visitors. Under the direction of Hans Maier some changes to the sets and the text are made for the sake of formal clarity and the message of the Play. Women who live in Oberammergau, are unmarried and under 35, win the passive and active right to vote on the committee.

1990   The thirty-ninth Passion Play. Although a new generation moves onto the local council in 1984, a decision is made in favour of the Weis–Daisenberger text. This is followed by the surprising election of the youngest ever director of the Play, namely the sculptor Christian Stückl, aged 27. During the preparatory phase leading up to the performances, a commission responsible for the text, headed by Prof. Rudolf Pesch, works on solutions to the queries raised by the Anti-Defamation League to combat anti-Semitism (again with Swidler and Sloyen).

Recognising the rights of sexual equality, following a case taken by three women from Oberammergau to the state court of Bavaria, both married women and those over 35 are now allowed to perform in the Play.

Christian Stückl assigns a number of major roles to younger actors. Debates about his leadership take on a dramatic character, but his dismissal can be narrowly averted. Nevertheless, following a signature campaign, the committee bows to the popular opinion of the conservative fraction and withdraws its previously granted approval of Alexander Kraut's stage set. (480,000 visitors).

"Who needs witnesses? He has blasphemed God", the Interrogation before Caiaphus scene, directed by Christian Stückl, 1990

Crucifixion scene, directed by Christian Stückl, 1990

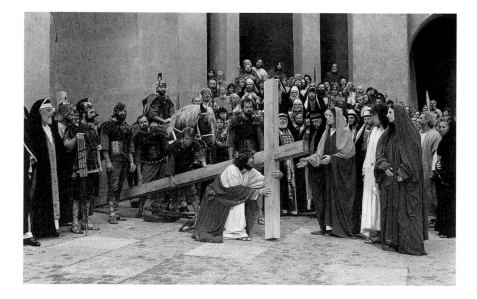

2000 The fortieth Passion Play. In just the same way as theologians discuss the most suitable wording to be used by God and His son, artists continue to ponder the never-ending problem of how best to convey the religious essence of the Play, the debate about fulfilling the task in hand in an optimum way, be it traditional or contemporary, is part and parcel of Oberammergau. And this does not shy away from any social or politcal conflict. Since the inclusion of a new political tool – the local referendum – Oberammergau has become the parish with the most declarations of intent in Bavaria!

– Declaration of intent no. 1: Rosner vs. Daisenberger as the basis of the text for the year 2000. The decision falls in 1996 in favour of the latter.

– Declarations of intent nos. 2 and 3: Should Christian Stückl remain director of the Play? In 1997, the Stückl camp wins the vote, the conservative camp, around Dr. Rudolf Zwink, loses.

– Declaration of intent no. 4: Should the traditional appearance of the exterior façades of the Passion Play Theatre be left as they are, or clad in wood in a sober but modern style? In 1997 the decision falls in favour of the former.

In addition, a motion is also passed by the council: should the right to participate be changed to include those living in Oberammergau who are not Christian or not German? The result is positive.

In 1997, an agreement is also made with the Catholic Church. The Cardinal of the Archdiocese Munich-Freising undertakes to become the patron of the Passion Play on the condition that the person appointed by him approve the production of the Play and the text in particular.

In the same year, the council commissions Christian Stückl with the task of preparing a new production for which Stefan Hageneier is to create both the stage sets and the costumes, Markus Zwink to compose the music and Otto Huber to revise the text. Spread out over 1997/98, the results are presented in stages to the council and the local clergy, the theologian, Prof. Ludwig Mödl, appointed by Cardinal Wetter and Bishop von Löwenich, and are unanimously approved by the council.

The Orchestra

Acknowledgments

Our special thanks go to Hans Schwaighofer for letting us publish extracts of his work for the Rosner production, to Hella Wolf-Lang for lending pictorial material in her ownership and to the director of the Archive of the Archdiocese of Munich and Freising, Dr. Peter Pfister, for photographs of the parish register. Our sincere gratitude also goes to Helmut W. Klinner who, once again, has let us search through the extensive material in the Community of Oberammergau Archives and who was always on hand to help us find the treasured pieces we were looking for. Last and by no means least, we would like to thank our editors, Gabriele Ebbecke and Christopher Wynne, for their much valued advice and exceptional commitment.

Photographic credits:
pp. 7–15: Tomas Dashuber, Munich
pp. 17–144, 159: Brigitte Maria Mayer, Berlin
p. 145 top: The Archive of the Archdiocese of Munich and Freising
p. 145 bottom: The Community of Oberammergau Archives (GAO)
p. 146 top: The Benedictine Abbey, Ettal
p. 146 bottom–p. 152 top: GAO
p. 152 bottom: Hella Wolf-Lang, Oberammergau
p. 153–p. 154 top: GAO
p. 154 bottom and p. 155: private ownership,
        Hans Schwaighofer, Oberammergau
pp. 156, 157: GAO (photos: Thomas Klinger)